Wacky Trees

Wacky Trees

D. M. Souza

Franklin Watts
A Division of Scholastic Inc.
New York • Toronto • London • Auckland • Sydney
Mexico City • New Delhi • Hong Kong
Danbury, Connecticut

Note to readers: Definitions for words in **bold** can be found in the Glossary at the back of this book.

Photographs © 2003: Dembinsky Photo Assoc.: 29 (Dominique Braud), 11 (Mary Clay), 14 (Bill Lea), 15 (Doug Locke); Hunt Institute for Botanical Documentation: 20; Peter Arnold Inc.: 42 (Fred Bruemmer), 22 (Michael Fairchild), 10 (Walter H. Hodge), 23 (Steve Kaufman), 26, 40 (Norbert Wu), cover (Gunter Ziesler); Photo Researchers, NY: 32 (Mark N. Boulton), 5 left, 31 (Gregory G. Dimijian), 8, 48 (Dennis Flaherty), 53 (Fletcher & Baylis), 47 (F. Gohier), 16 (Ken M. Johns), 2 (Hubertus Kanus), 5 right, 18 (S.R. Maglione), 6 (John Mead/SPL), 30 (Beatrice Neff), 34 (F. Stuart Westmorland), 12 (George Whiteley), 36 (Terry Whittaker); Visuals Unlimited: 38 (David S. Addison), 13 (Jack M. Bostrack), 44, 51 (D. Cavagnaro), 21 (Gerald & Buff Corsi), 46 (John D. Cunningham), 25 (Carlyn Galati), 24 (Prance), 9 (John Sohlden), 37 (Richard Thom).

The photograph opposite the title page shows a baobab tree.

Library of Congress Cataloging-in-Publication Data

Souza, D. M. (Dorothy M.)
    Wacky trees / D.M. Souza.
        p. cm. — (Watts library)
    Summary: Explores strange trees, including the baobab, strangler fig, mangrove, boojum, and bristlecone pine.
    Includes bibliographical references (p.   ).
    ISBN 0-531-12210-7 (lib. bdg.)   0-531-16246-X (pbk.)
    1. Trees—Juvenile literature. [1. Trees.] I. Title. II. Series.
QK475.8 .S68 2003
582.16—dc21

2001008286

Contents

This massive sequoia is growing in the Sequoia National Park, California.

Chapter One

Vital Parts

Have you ever climbed a tree or swung from its sturdy branches? Perhaps on a hot summer day you've cooled yourself under the shade of a giant oak. But did you know that trees provide many other benefits? Their leaves soak up vast amounts of carbon dioxide from the atmosphere. These same leaves filter and trap smoke, dust, and ash, and give off oxygen every creature needs. Many trees furnish food and shelter for humans and animals. They also supply us with hundreds of useful products. Actually, trees play an indispensable role in the lives of countless living organisms on Earth.

Record Holders

A giant sequoia tree, growing on the western slope of the Sierra Nevada mountains, is the most massive living organism on Earth. A 367-foot (112-meter) redwood tree on the Pacific coast is the tallest living tree, and a bristlecone pine in the White Mountains of California is the oldest. The bristlecone began growing at the same time the great pyramids were being constructed in Egypt.

Thousands of different **species** of trees grow around the world. Some, such as pines and firs, have needlelike leaves. Others, such as oaks and maples, have broad, flat leaves. A number of species are strange looking, have unusual features, or are record holders. Yet all trees possess the same basic parts: roots, trunks, and leaves. Before spotlighting a few of the wacky varieties, let's briefly examine the almost magical way in which trees function.

Underground Operations

Every tree growing in a forest, park, or on a street corner has a root system to anchor its aboveground structure. This system is constantly searching for water and nutrients. The majority of roots are hidden in the top 12 to 18 inches (30 to 46 centimeters) of soil, where water and rich decomposing matter accumulate. Able to divide again and again, many roots spread like underground branches, with some extending two to four times beyond the spread of aboveground branches.

The root system of a tree such as this bur oak may spread almost as far as its aboveground branches.

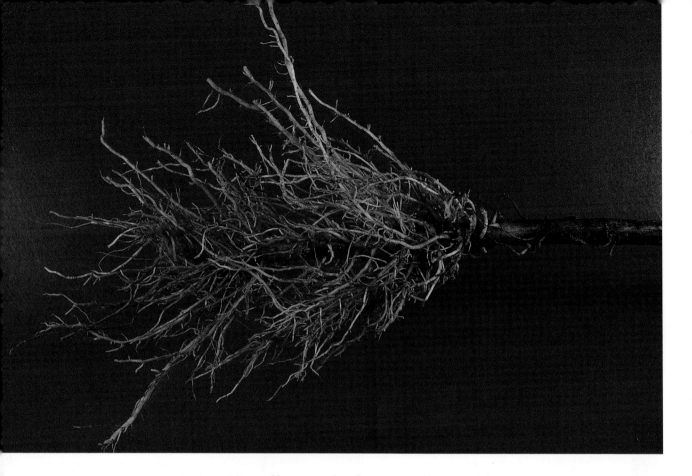

Flowers as well as trees have fibrous roots that search for food. These belong to a zinnia.

Not all roots do the same thing. **Fibrous roots** are feeding roots, and their most vital parts are their tips that measure about 1 inch (2.5 cm) long and are as thin as string. Protected by a thimblelike cap, these tips are the only parts of the feeding roots that grow in length. As they push through the soil, dodging rocks and other hard objects, masses of tiny white root hairs behind them absorb water and dissolved minerals. While the hairs attach themselves to soil, the tips push for-

Zapping Competition

The roots of some trees, such as those of the black walnut, release chemicals that prevent other trees and plants from growing nearby.

10

ward, searching for new supplies. Root hairs work for a time, then die, but are constantly being replaced.

Some trees, such as oaks, hickories, and walnuts, also have a strong central root that can plunge more than 15 feet (4.5 m) into the ground like an upside-down trunk. This **taproot** helps stabilize the trees and keeps them from toppling in a storm. Other trees have large roots closer to the surface that provide support.

Inner Workings

Surrounding the trunk of a tree is its bark, a tough skin that protects the inner parts of the tree from drying out and from being damaged by insects, disease, and injuries. The outer bark can be less than .5 inch (1.25 cm) or more than 29 inches (74 cm) thick. The bark sometimes helps identify different species of trees. For example, white birch bark peels off like paper. Shagbark hickory looks like house shingles, and the bark of cork oak can be removed in large sheets. It is used to make cork products.

The red-brown bark of the Texas madrone turns scaly and peels off as the tree ages.

Beneath the outer bark is a network of tiny tubes serving as supply lines for the entire tree. One set of tubes lies in the **phloem**, or inner bark, and carries sugars and other substances from the leaves to various parts of the tree. Each year a layer of phloem dies and becomes part of the slowly thickening outer bark.

Next to the inner bark is the **cambium**, a paper-thin layer of cells. During spring and summer, as cambium cells divide, some become a new layer of phloem. Others turn into new wood known as **xylem**.

Running through the xylem are additional tubes that carry water and dissolved minerals from the roots to the leaves. The new wood is porous, moist, and marked with light rings pro-

Parts of a trunk easy to identify are the outer bark, inner bark (phloem), cambium, and heartwood.

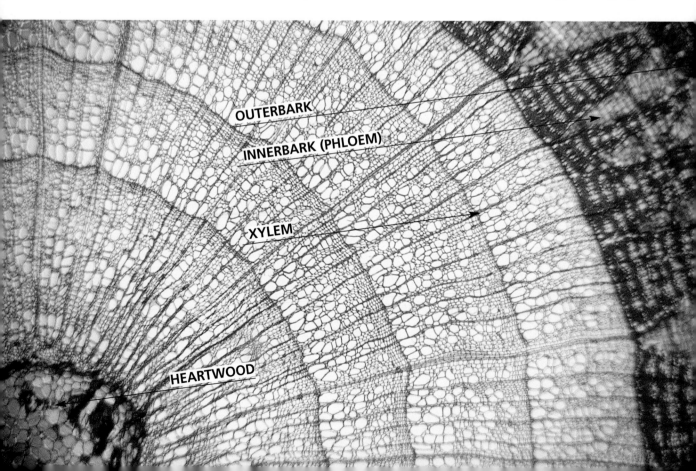

OUTERBARK

INNERBARK (PHLOEM)

XYLEM

HEARTWOOD

Record Keeping

It is not necessary to cut down a tree to determine its age. A special instrument called an **increment borer** can remove a sample of inner wood about the width of a soda straw without damaging the tree. By comparing the sample from one tree to those from surrounding trees, scientists can often gain clues about droughts, wildfires, and other events that have affected the trees in the past.

duced in spring and dark ones produced in summer. One set of light and dark rings often represents a year's growth. Scientists count these rings when trying to determine a tree's age.

Eventually, a number of tubes in the inner wood become clogged with liquid and turn into **heartwood**, the dark center of the trunk. If fungi or insects invade, the heartwood may decay. Although the tree continues to appear normal and may remain standing for years, it is in danger of falling at any time.

Production Zone

Rising from the trunk of the tree and reaching toward sunlight is the **crown**, a multitude of branches, twigs, and leaves. Whether thin and flat like a maple leaf, or narrow and round like a pine needle, all leaves perform the same important task. They make food for the tree. Using water pulled from the roots, carbon dioxide from the air, and energy from the Sun,

Fast growing yellow poplar trees have been used to absorb toxic chemicals from the soil and release them in the form of harmless vapor.

they manufacture a simple sugar solution that fuels the tree. The process is known as **photosynthesis**, a Greek word meaning "to put together with light."

Surprisingly, although leaves receive huge amounts of water from roots, they use only a small amount. Through pinpoint openings covering their surface, they expel the excess as vapor. On a summer day some large trees release hundreds of gallons of water vapor that help cool the surrounding area. The leaves also release oxygen, which all animals need.

A portion of the food made by leaves provides energy for the growth of various parts of the tree. Another portion is stored for later use or helps form flowers, fruits, and seeds needed for the next generation of trees. Some food also helps produce products that humans find useful. A few of these are listed in the table (page 17).

Trees are not merely structures for climbing and swinging, or "factories" producing a variety of goods. They are

This sugar maple leaf catches sunlight, and its strong veins bring water to the leaf and carry food to the rest of the tree.

Quick Replacements

When water vapor is released from leaves, more water is pulled from the soil into the roots and up through the xylem tubes to the leaves. In certain trees, this water moves upward at the rate of almost 150 feet (45 m) an hour.

Masquerading as trees in the desert are these yuccas, members of the Lily family.

dynamic organisms finely tuned to their environments. Each year, as millions of insects attack them, birds roost or nest in them, and armies of other animals use and abuse them in many ways, the roots, trunks, and leaves of many trees continue to function. In lush rain forests where sunlight is limited, or on high mountain peaks where wind, heat, and cold are extreme, trees adapt. When soil becomes poor or seasons bring little or too much water, they survive. However, in their struggles some of these trees become as weird and wacky-looking as the ones we are about to meet.

Products from Trees

Product	Tree	Use
Aspirin	Willow	Painkiller originally obtained from bark of willow
Chicle	Sapodilla	Main ingredient of chewing gum
Chocolate	Cacao	Beverage, candy
Coffee	Coffee	Beverage
Latex	Rubber	At one time, the only source of rubber for tires
Nutmeg	Nutmeg	Spice
Quinine	Cinchona	Medicine used to cure malaria
Turpentine	Pine	Paint thinner, solvent

Baobab trees dominate the landscape wherever they grow.

Chapter Two

Upside-Down Giants

According to an African legend, the gods planted a large tree in the rain forests of the Congo. One day, the tree complained that the moisture of the place was making its trunk swell, so the gods moved it to East Africa's Mountains of the Moon. When the tree continued to complain, the gods tossed it into a dry area where it landed upside down. This is why, according to the legend tellers, the African baobab tree now appears to have roots growing in the air.

Behind the Name

Michél Adanson, a French botanist (1727–1806) who lived in Senegal for several years, was the first to describe the tree in detail. In 1759, Carolus Linnaeus, the Swedish physician and naturalist who introduced the system for classifying all living organisms, honored Adanson by giving the baobab the scientific name *Adansonia digitata*.

One look at the baobab and it is easy to see how fantastic tales sprang up around it. Leaves extend like the fingers of a hand and are clustered at the ends of short, stocky branches. When the tree is leafless it looks like an upside-down giant.

Ranging in height from 16 to 100 feet (5 to 30 m), baobabs are not exceptionally tall. Their trunks, however, are massive. Some are bottle-shaped and measure 35 feet (10.5 m) in diameter.

Michél Adanson was the first botanist to scientifically describe the baobab tree.

Relatives

The baobab belongs to the Bombacaceae family of trees. Other members of this family that are economically important are the kapok tree, a source of stuffing for pillows and jackets, and the balsa tree, useful in building rafts and model airplanes.

Some baobab trees in Madagascar are believed to be the dwelling places of spirits.

Binomials

All living things have a two-part scientific name, or **binomial**. The first gives the genus to which the organism belongs, and the second, the species, identifies the particluar organism within the genus.

Twenty to forty adult humans can move around easily inside some trunks. Other baobabs are tapered like a candle and have multiple barrels or bottle shapes that branch off near the ground.

The enormous size of the trunks has led some people to suspect that the trees are thousands of years old. Because their

Baobabs not only attract birds, bats, monitors, and geckos, but also children who enjoying playing in and around them.

inner wood is often missing or is pulpy and lacks rings, there is no reliable way to determine how old they are. Scientists have tried to determine the approximate ages of dead baobabs. Using **carbon dating** on a tree with a trunk 15 feet (4.5 m) in diameter, they estimated it to be more than 2,000 years old.

Secrets of Survival

The extensive root systems of the baobabs have adapted to barren land and can draw out the slightest bits of moisture from the soil. The trees conserve energy by shedding foliage during the dry season. Some do not bloom until they are twenty years old.

During midsummer, which is December in southern Africa, fragrant flowers appear on some baobab trees. They have large, white, waxy petals and hang down on long stalks. The blooms open at night when bats, long-tongued hawkmoths, and nocturnal lemurs pollinate them. Within twenty four hours they wilt and fall to the ground.

The fruits that eventually appear on the tree are about 12 inches (30 cm) long and are covered with velvety hairs. Some look like sausages hanging from barren branches. The fruit of one is thought to resemble dead rats hanging by their tails. "Dead rat tree" is the common name for this tree.

When they are about forty years of age, the trunks of baobabs begin to

Fragrant white blooms of the baobab open when the sun sets and attract bats, which pollinate them.

Superstitions

Some people believe that spirits inhabit the flowers of the baobab and that a lion will eat anyone who picks the blooms.

The fruit of some baobabs look like dead rats hanging by their tails.

swell. Each year after that their size increases and, because of their pulpy interiors, people frequently hollow them out for water storage. A single tree has been estimated to hold as many as 31,000 gallons (117,490 liters) of water.

Superstore

Few tropical trees are used in as many ways as the baobab. Fiber, pounded from the bark of its lower trunk, is used to make rope, baskets, cloth, and string for musical instruments. Although this practice would likely lead to the death of other trees, it does little harm to the baobab. Leaves, high in vitamins A and C, are eaten fresh or in soups. Some people use them to treat kidney and bladder disease as well as asthma and insect bites. The seeds of several species are considered a treat, and cooking oil is often extracted from them.

A variety of creatures visit baobabs. Hornbills, owls, parrots, and other birds make their nests in the branches. Kangaroos, elephants, and baboons feed on different parts. Animals and people often seek shelter in the deep trunk cavities.

Another species of baobab (*Adansonia gregorii*) was discovered in Australia in the middle of the 19th century. In addition

Jailhouse

Early pioneers in Australia sometimes carved an opening in the trunk of a baobab, removed the pulp, then lit a fire to dry the area. Grates were placed over the openings and prisoners were locked inside. Some of these former jailhouses are still standing today.

to the African and Australian varieties, six species have been identified in Madagascar. Baobabs have also been planted in the tropical regions of India, South America, and even in southern Florida and the Caribbean, where they have become attention-grabbers.

Baboons, monkeys, and elephants enjoy eating baobab fruit and spread seeds in their droppings.

The Spanish word for the strangler fig is matapalo, *which means killer tree.*

Chapter Three

The Stranglers

The air cackles with the screeches and calls of wild birds. Black mynahs, parrots, hornbills, and other feathery residents of the rain forest clamor for feeding positions on trees loaded with golf-ball-sized red figs. One hornbill lands on a branch, plucks a fig with its beak, and carries it back to a nest in the canopy of another tree. Each day after its chicks are fed the soft juicy treats, the indigestible fig seeds fall below their nest.

One day, a seed lands in the moist crevice of a branch. It germinates, and in time, nourished by rain, air, and dust, begins growing as an **epiphyte**. Searching for water and nutrients, it sends out thin aerial roots. These roots twist and turn slowly downward around the tree like vines until they reach the ground below. Gradually, they grow thicker, stronger, and harder, until one day each one is like a trunk. Tighter and tighter they wind around their host, suffocating it in their deadly grip. They become a tree known as a strangler, or *matapalo*, which means killer.

Of the many stranglers that grow around the world, most are figs belonging to the same family as mulberry trees (Moraceae). Stranglers are native in every tropical area except the Hawaiian Islands. Some are sacred to people in India, China, and parts of Southeast Asia. Many provide food and shelter for a variety of animals.

Deadly Grip

If the seed of a strangler falls to the ground in the middle of the rain forest, it usually germinates but does not live long, due to the deep shade of surrounding trees. But if it begins its life high in the branches of another tree, it is able to overcome this handicap. Unfortunately, the future of its host is not as bright.

Once a strangler encircles another tree, it can crush that tree's outer bark and cut off the supply line of food running through its inner bark. Eventually, the support tree dies. This

Ancient Paper

Aztec and Mayan peoples took thin strips of bark from strangler figs, pounded them with a stone, and turned them into paper.

Roots of the strangler grow down from branches of a host tree and gradually strangle the host.

is why the strangler is sometimes referred to as the boa constrictor of the plant world.

The roots of strangler figs can force their way between limestone blocks of buildings and other structures. Many ancient Mayan cities have been destroyed or reduced to rubble as a result of these trees. In Coral Gables, Florida, the roots of several stranglers have buckled pavement as well as crushed concrete swimming pools.

Tourist Attractions

In north Queensland, Australia, the seed of one fig (*Ficus virens*) landed in the branches of a tree and sprouted. Before its roots could reach the ground the support tree toppled and landed on a neighboring tree. The roots of the strangler simply detoured away from the leaning trunk until they reached

Cool Shade

Legend has it that Alexander the Great once camped with an army of 7,000 men under the shade of a banyan.

the ground. In time, they thickened and hardened, and when the support tree rotted away, the so-called Curtain Fig stood in its place. Visitors from around the world come to marvel at this famous strangler's bizarre shape, which resembles a giant curtain.

One of the largest strangler figs is the banyan. When its roots reach the ground, they serve as props supporting the whole structure. More than 1,775 **prop roots** were counted on a banyan growing in the Calcutta Botanic Garden in India. Another banyan growing east of Bombay, India, has a crown

The Curtain Fig, growing in Queensland, Australia, attracts visitors from around the world.

that extends over several acres and has more than 3,000 prop roots. What appears to be a forest of trees is actually a single tree.

Popular Hangouts

Monkeys spend hours in strangler trees eating the ripe fruit and napping.

Once its support tree rots and its interior becomes hollow, the stranglers' roots serve as a living ladder that tree dwellers use to climb into its branches. When fruit ripens, monkeys spend hours in the tree. They munch, nap for a while, then wake to

begin munching again. One black macaque was clocked eating 140 figs a minute.

Squirrels and hundreds of birds also feast on the sweet treats or rest in the cool shade, especially on hot days. Geckos, frogs, lizards, bees, wasps, beetles, and ants visit the tree or make their home in it during different parts of the year. At night, flocks of fruit-eating bats swoop into the branches for a feast.

One of the smallest creatures to use the strangler fig is a tiny wasp. As soon as unripe figs appear on its branches, swarms of female wasps arrive with pollen and wriggle through pinpoint openings at one end of each fig. They lay their eggs in developing flowers inside each fig and then die. Soon after, their young hatch. They then mate, and upon leaving, take pollen with them to the next fig tree. In this way, the cycle begins all over again. Without these tiny wasps to act as pollinators, the stranglers could not supply forest creatures with one of their most important sources of nourishment.

Salt water is lethal to most plants but not to these mangrove trees growing in the Caribbean Sea.

Chapter Four

Smart Roots

A small, egg-shaped object with a spearlike root falls from a tree and lands in the water. For weeks, it bobs along the surface of the sea until a current carries it close to shore. As soon as its root touches bottom, it begins growing. In twenty-five to thirty years, a thick forest of impenetrable trees, known as mangroves, may surround this single pioneer seedling.

More than fifty species of mangroves grow worldwide along the edges of the sea. Some reach 80-feet (24 m) in height. Three mangrove species are common along the southern coasts of Florida: the

Largest Forest

The Sundarbans, the largest man-grove forest, lies along coastal India and Bangladesh and is home to the famous Royal Bengal Tiger.

white (*Laguncularia racemosa*), the black, (*Avicennia germinans*), and the red (*Rhizophora mangle*).

Beating the Odds

Fingerlike pneuma-tophores help the roots of black mangroves obtain oxygen.

Most trees cannot survive in salt water, which in high levels can be toxic to them. Also, they have a difficult time rooting in unstable sand and are unable to find the oxygen they need.

However, both the black and the red mangroves have adapted to such difficult environments in fascinating ways.

During high tides, the roots of black mangroves are often underwater. To obtain oxygen, they send up a mass of finger-like structures known as **pneumatophores**. Hundreds of these air-breathing growths may surround the trunks of many trees. Meanwhile, underwater roots filter salt from the water and, if any enters the xylem, special glands in the leaves evaporate the excess. Sometimes, salt crystals can be seen on leaf surfaces.

"Walking Trees"

The red mangrove is probably the most easily recognized of all the mangroves. From March to November, hundreds of inchwide, pale yellow flowers bloom on each mature tree. After the blossoms fall, leathery, brown, seed-filled fruit, about the size of plums, develop in their place.

Unlike the seeds of other trees that must land on moist soil before sprouting, the seeds of most mangroves sprout while still on the tree. Root ends appear first, then stems. These **propagules**, as they are called, grow between 10 and 12 inches (25 and 30 cm) long and resemble small spears or daggers before falling into the water. Being heavier than the rest of the seed, the sharp root tip takes hold. Some propagules begin growing near their parent, but others drift thousands of miles away before taking root.

Red Water

The bark of the red mangrove contains a natural dye that is used to stain floors and furniture. Sometimes, the water around the trees turns red.

Mangrove propagules may drift thousands of miles before taking root.

Tracing Roots

Scientists believe that some red mangrove trees growing along the coasts of Florida may have descended from seeds that floated all the way from East Africa.

Once rooted, the red mangrove seedlings send out a network of small roots that arch above the waterline. They resemble stilts or the long, thin legs of wading shore birds and give the illusion that the trees are "walking" on the water. Plunging a foot or more into the sandy seafloor, they help anchor and support the trees against the pull of tides. Blisterlike structures on their above-water side draw in oxygen, and special root cells filter salt from their water supply. By the time the trees are three or four years old, prop roots appear and continue reaching out until they become a thick tangle. Leaves, bark, sea grasses, and other debris caught in the root maze are gradually broken down by bacteria, fungi, and a variety of sea animals. Slowly, they build up a thick layer of rich soil around them where other mangrove seedlings are able to take root.

Red mangrove trees grow throughout tropical America and are the best known of Florida's species.

Mangroves' prop roots protect coastlines against erosion and the action of waves. They filter dirt and pollutants from storm runoffs and provide habitats for a variety of animals. Their forests are unique **ecosystems.**

Hideouts

Branches of the red mangrove are nesting, perching, and roosting sites for hundreds of birds such as pelicans, herons, snowy egrets, and cormorants. By day, some of the birds dive into the water searching for a meal. At night, others feed on

Many creatures hang out in and around red mangroves.

flying insects that swarm over the water. Tree snakes lie in wait for birds, small rodents, or tree frogs, and raccoons poke among the roots searching for crabs and other shellfish.

Beneath the surface of the water, oysters cling to the sturdy tree roots. Shrimp, crabs, and many small worms nibble on decomposing leaves that have fallen into the water. Fish of every size and color swim around searching for a meal. Occasionally, a sea horse will curl the tip of its tail around a stem, or an alligator, trailing a large fish, will enter the mangrove area and send other sea life scurrying for cover.

Oyster Bars

Living oysters and the shells of dead ones form oyster bars that mangrove trees and their tangled roots turn into islands.

Too Useful

Mangroves protect shorelines and provide habitat for a host of animals. The trees also produce many useful products. In different parts of the world, the wood of the mangrove tree is turned into fuel for heating and cooking. Because it is strong and water resistant, it is in demand for building houses, boats, and furniture. Its resistance to rot and attacks by fungi makes it ideal for the construction of underwater structures. Charcoal and wood chips can also be made from mangroves.

In Malaysia, pneumatophores are used for baskets, corks, and floats. In Sri Lanka, pulp is turned into paper, matchsticks, toys, and other products. In India, tannin in the bark is used to cure leather. Furniture stain and dyes are also made from bark extracts. Mangroves have been successful in adapting to harsh environments, but the many useful products they provide may play a role in hastening their disappearance.

Some boojum trees look like spiny candles towering over the desert.

Chapter Five

Desert Oddities

Lewis Carroll, in his poem, *The Hunting of the Snark*, describes a far-off land inhabited by a strange creature called the "boojum." In 1922, Godfrey Sykes, an English adventurer, along with a group of scientists from the Desert Botanical Laboratory in Tucson, Arizona, were searching for plants in the Sonoran Desert. At one point, Sykes aimed his telescope at something strange growing on a rocky slope. Remembering Carroll's poem, he immediately called it a "boojum." The fanciful name has been used ever since.

Unusual plants dot the desert areas of Mexico, but the boojum (*Idria columnaris*) is more bizarre than all the others. It looks more like a monstrous spiny candle than a living tree. Actually, its Spanish name, *cirio*, means tall candle.

The winds can twist boojums into incredible shapes.

Boojumland

The boojum is a member of the Fouquieriaceae family. All the members of this family are spiny and grow only in deserts or other dry areas of Mexico and the southwestern United States. Thick stands of boojums growing more than 60 feet (18 m) tall can be found on the central Baja peninsula. Smaller populations grow along the rocky coastline of Sonora, Mexico. Here they seldom reach more than 40 feet (12 m) tall, as winds from the sea bend their trunks into strangely contorted shapes. Some even grow close to the ground or twist and loop in the air.

Millions of years ago, the area where the first boojum grew was wet and lush. As the land became more

Bad Luck Tree

The Seri Indians of the Sonoran coast tell of a tidal wave that once washed over the land of their ancestors. As the wave retreated, the men were turned into tall boojum trees and the women into short ones. The belief is that if anyone harms one of these "bad luck" trees, a sudden storm or other catastrophe will strike the area.

desertlike, the boojum adapted. It collected and stored every bit of moisture, even dew and fog, in its trunk. Since then its appearance has changed little.

Winter Grower

Although it is a tree, the boojum is also a **succulent**, or water-storing plant. It has a main stem or trunk protected by a grayish-white bark tough enough to keep rodents from eating through to the water-storing tissues inside. Some boojums split into two or more stems near the top. Pencil-thin branches, armed with spines like a cactus, cover the length of the stems. Few animals use the tree as either food or shelter, although some raptors are known to build their nests in the branches.

Annual Rainfall

Some years, 5 inches (13 cm) of rain fall in boojumland. Other years, there may be no rain at all.

For most of the year, the boojum is **dormant**, but during the first rains small, rounded leaves appear on its branches. To preserve moisture, these leaves soon wither and fall to the ground, and in their place spines and small buds develop. If rains come again, a second crop of leaves may appear above the spines.

45

Pencil thin branches of boojums are covered with prickly spines.

From July to September, fragrant yellow or white blossoms appear at the top of the tree and are pollinated by insects, hummingbirds, and bats. Winds carry seeds to new grounds, but without sufficient moisture few seeds are able to become new trees. A crop of seeds may be successful only once every twenty-five years.

Slow Pokes

The boojum is a slow grower taking about ten to twenty years to reach 12 inches (30 cm) in height. The tree may not flower until it is one hundred years old. Some scientists once believed that the tallest trees were several hundred years old. More

46

recently, however, the age of the oldest specimen has been estimated to be 1,000 years old.

In 1970, Robert Humphrey from the University of Arizona found the tallest boojum yet discovered. It was growing near the Gulf of California. At the time, it was 81 feet (24 m) tall. Twenty-eight years later, the boojum and the plants surrounding it were gone. It is believed that Hurricane Nora, which struck the area in September 1997, swept them away.

Although strong winds sometimes claim a few trees, most remain safe. Because their wood is useless as firewood, and because animals do not find them inviting, the trees are left to grow at their own slow pace. Also, thanks to the efforts of Humphrey, all of central Baja California, is now a national park, and Mexican law protects the trees. Fortunately, these desert oddities will continue to amaze spectators for many years.

Fragrant flowers appear in clusters at the tips of boojums.

The twisted and gnarled trunks of bristlecones sometimes look like living driftwood.

Chapter Six

Survivors

Most trees cannot grow above 11,000 feet (3,355 m). Gale-force winds and blasts of cold, dry air sweep over the landscape and turn plants into twisted dwarfs. Yet in this environment, some of the oldest trees on Earth manage to survive. Some of their secrets were discovered in the 20th century.

Tracking Methuselah

In 1953, Edmund Schulman, a scientist studying the rings of trees in Sun Valley, Idaho, found a timber pine that proved to be 1,700 years old. Hearing that even older trees were growing on the White Mountains in California, Schulman and a colleague decided to explore the area. In 1957, the two men made the journey up the mountains to above 10,000 feet (3,050 m). Here, in poor soil and harsh conditions, they found several twisted and contorted bristlecone pines (*Pinus logaeva*) that looked more dead than alive. Closer examination proved that one tree was more than 4,000 years old. Schulman named it Pine Alpha. Another tree, called Methuselah, was discovered to be 4,723 years old. It came to be known as the world's oldest **conifer**.

At about the same time, members of a group calling themselves the Great Basin National Park Association claimed that the bristlecones of Wheeler Peak, Nevada, were older than those in California. In 1964, Donald R. Currey, a university student, traveled to Wheeler Peak with a friend and took core samples from some of the trees. Before their work could be completed their increment borer broke, and they asked permission of the U.S.D.A. Forest Service to cut down a bristlecone in order to count its rings. Permission was granted. Eventually, the men determined its age to be more than 4,800 years, but tragically they had destroyed the tree in order to make this discovery.

Clever Tactics

The oldest bristlecone pines still grow where few other plants can. The soil surrounding their roots holds few nutrients and looks more like the surface of the moon than an earthly

Memorial

Soon after his discoveries, Dr. Schulman died. In 1958 the U.S.D.A. Forest Service established the Ancient Bristlecone Pine Forest in the White Mountains and named a special area the Schulman Grove in honor of the scientist.

landscape. Yet the bristlecones have survived in such places for centuries. How do they do it?

In early May, as the hours of sunlight increase, snow on the mountains surrounding the trees begins to melt. During the six to eight weeks of warmer weather, new twigs and cones appear. Bristlecones do not spend much energy forming new

The bristlecone tree is named for the brownish scales on its cones, which are tipped with thin, curved bristles.

needles, since theirs can live twenty to thirty years. If fire, lightning, or sudden storms strike, portions of their bark and new wood die back. This dieback saves more of the trees' energy by reducing the amount of nutrients they need to produce.

The trees can reach 60 feet (18 m) in height, but usually grow to only about 30 feet (10 m) with twisted and gnarled trunks. They grow slowly, taking about a hundred years to add 1 inch (2.5 cm) to their trunks' diameter. Dense bark and thick resins prevent invasions by bacteria, fungi, and insects. Even after a tree dies, it can remain standing for hundreds of years. The dryness of the air surrounding it keeps its wood from rotting, and wind and ice continually polish its bark to a fine finish.

Missing Link

Another unusual tree or treelike plant is surviving in a different kind of harsh environment. In 1859, Dr. Friedrich Welwitsch, an Austrian botanist, discovered strange objects growing in the Namib Desert in southwestern Africa. Each one had a short, cracked wooden trunk that looked like the heartwood of most trees. Two flat, stiff, olive-green leaves grew from the trunk in opposite directions and sprawled several hundred square feet over the desert floor. Some of the leaves were split and frayed at their tips as a result of being tossed about by winds. Dr. Welwitsch was awestruck by the peculiar growths.

Dying Young

Bristlecones grow taller and faster at lower elevations, but they die after 300 or 400 years. It seems that the more difficult the growing conditions, the longer the trees live.

Since the discovery of *Welwitschia mirabilis*, as the plants were later called, scientists have been trying to determine what the plants are and how they survive in an area where rainfall averages only 1 inch (2.5 cm) annually. Leaves, several of which according to carbon dating are 1,500 years old, are never shed but grow about 5 inches (13 cm) each year. While other plants adapt to the lack of moisture by reducing their leaf size, *Welwitschia* does not. Instead, it absorbs drops of fog through millions of tiny pores on the surface of each giant leaf.

The woody trunk has a large taproot that reaches deep under the surface of the soil. It also has many shallow roots.

The sprawling leaves of Welwitschia grow throughout the life of the plant and may live for more than 1,000 years.

Popular Names

Bushmen call *Welwitschia* "N'tumbo," or the "stump." Another common name is tree tumbo.

Under the shade of the giant leaves the soil remains cool and moist even in the heat of the day. Snakes, lizards, scorpions, spiders, and beetles all take refuge at this oasis in the desert.

Some scientists believe that *Welwitschia* might be the missing link between cone-bearing trees and broad-leaved ones. The plants have characteristics of both types: flowerlike structures as well as male and female cones. Several researchers, however, believe that *Welwitschia* is more closely related to conifers than anything else. Its place in the plant world may be debated for many years, but one thing is certain: *Welwitschia* definitely belongs on a list of the weirdest-looking trees on Earth.

The greatest threat to all these strange and wacky trees comes not from their surroundings but from the humans who visit them each year. The location of Methuselah, for example, remains unmarked to protect it from vandals. Only if these ancient wonders are allowed to grow undisturbed can they continue to provide us with links to the past.

Glossary

binomial—a two-part scientific name that indicates the genus and species of an organism

cambium—a thin layer of cells between the bark and the wood that produces more bark and wood

carbon dating—method of determining the age of an organism by comparing the amount of radioactive carbon (C14) with the amount of normal carbon in its tissues

conifer—a needle-leaved, usually evergreen, cone-bearing tree or shrub

crown—the branches, twigs, and leaves of a tree

dormant—inactive, with no growth

ecosystem—a community of organisms and its physical environment

epiphyte—a plant that grows on or in another plant, which serves as a support

fibrous root—a small feeding root of a tree or other plant

heartwood—the dense, dark wood at the center of a tree

increment borer—a tool used to remove a sample of wood from the center of a tree

phloem—the inner bark of a tree

photosynthesis—the process by which leaves, using energy from the Sun, change water and carbon dioxide into sugars

pneumatophore—a special growth on the roots of mangroves that helps them obtain oxygen and carbon dioxide

prop root—a root that supports the framework of certain trees

propagule—any part of a plant that can grow into a new plant

species—a group of closely related organisms

succulent—a plant with water-storing tissues

taproot—a deep root that helps anchor trees and other plants

xylem—the water-conducting part of a plant; in trees it is what we call wood

To Find Out More

Books

Bash, Barbara. *The Tree of Life: The World of the African Baobab.* Boston: Little, Brown and Company, 1989.

Cassie, Brian. *National Audubon Society First Field Guide: Trees.* New York: Scholastic, 1999.

Kneidel, Sally. *Skunk Cabbage, Sundew Plants and Strangler Figs, The Strangest Plants on Earth.* New York: John Wiley & Sons, 2001.

Lavies, Bianca. *Mangrove Wilderness, Nature's Nursery.* New York: Dutton Children's Books, 1994.

Pascoe, Elaine. *Leaves and Trees.* Woodbridge, Conn.: Blackbirch Press, 2001.

Videos and Images Online

California Gold. Huell Howser Productions, 1993.

Photosynthesis. Aims Media, 1994.

Trees: Evergreens and Deciduous. Aims Media, 1991.

http://www.sonic.net/bristlecone/Images.html
This site has a number of images of bristlecone pines.

http://www.namibstamps.com.na/welwitchia2000.htm
Four stamps show various images of *Welwitschia mirabilis*.

http://helios.bto.ed.ac.uk/bto/desbiome/boojum.htm
Images of boojum trees are featured here.

Organizations and Online Sites

Defenders of Wildlife
1101 14th St. NW, #1400
Washington, D.C. 20005
http://www.defenders.org
This organization helps protect native animals and plants in their natural habitats.

The Environmental Learning Center
255 Live Oak Drive
Vero Beach, FL 32963
http://indian-river.fl.us

The center is dedicated to protecting mangrove trees, especially in Indian River Lagoon, Florida.

International Society for Mangrove Ecosystems
University of the Ryukus
1 Senbaru Nishihara
903-0129 Okinawa
Japan
http://www.mangrove.or.jp/index.html/
The goal of this organization is to build information about various mangrove species and to distribute it globally.

The Nature Conservancy
4245 N. Fairfax Drive, Suite 100
Arlington, VA 22203
http://www.tnc.org
The purpose of this organization is to preserve native species and their habitats around the world.

The World Conservation Union
Rue Mauverney 28
1196 Gland
Switzerland
http://www.iucn.org/
This group encourages and assists societies around the world to conserve their natural environments and the species found in them.

A Note on Sources

When you live in an area surrounded by trees you begin to notice different things about them. Why do some shed bark at certain times of the year? Why do others look and grow the way they do? Two books from the local library helped answer a few of my questions: *Trees: Their Natural History* by Peter Thomas and *The Tree Book* by J. E. Milner. A third book, *Fantastic Trees* by E. A. Menninger, introduced me to a world of trees more bizarre than I could ever imagine.

Searching online sites, I found additional information on some of the unusual species mentioned in Menninger's work, as well as lists of recommended readings. *The Enchanted Canopy* by A. W. Mitchell, *Forest Giants of the World Past and Present* by A. Carder, *A Garden of Bristlecones* by Michael Cohen as well as numerous articles in magazines and scientific journals revealed even more about unusual trees. Visits to the sites where a few weird-looking ones grow capped my research for this book.

Index

Numbers in *italics* indicate illustrations.

About the Author

Reading about scientific developments and discoveries, exploring forests and seashores, observing wildlife, and introducing young people to the exciting world of nature are some of D.M. Souza's favorite things to do. As a freelancer she has written more than two dozen science-related books, including *Endangered Plants*, *Freaky Flowers*, *Meat-Eating Plants*, *Plant Invaders*, and *What Is a Fungus?* for Franklin Watts.